Learn Spanish Like a Native for Beginners - Level 2

Learning Spanish in Your Car Has Never Been Easier! Have Fun with Crazy Vocabulary, Daily Used Phrases, Exercises & Correct Pronunciations

www.LearnLikeNatives.com

© Copyright 2020 By Learn Like A Native

ALL RIGHTS RESERVED

No part of this book may be reproduced, stored in a retrieval system, or transmitted in any form or by any means, without the prior written permission of the publisher.

Content

Let me give you a little glance at what we will be seeing...

Introduction 1

Chapter 1 – Dreaming of the South 13

Chapter 2 – Not Only Birds Can Fly 33

Chapter 3 – Looking for a Ride? 43

Chapter 4 – I Find My Happiness Where the Sun Shines ... 55

Chapter 5 – I Have So Many Stories to Tell You 65

Chapter 6 – So Many Roads and So Many Places 86

Chapter 7 – Eat, Travel, Love 95

Chapter 8 – Sick & Abroad! 103

Chapter 9 – Learn the Ropes 110

Chapter 10 – Bring, Learn & Lead 119

Chapter 11 – New Job, New Life 131

Chapter 12 – Bringing Home the Bacon 139

Conclusion 147

Are you curious to discover more?

Introduction

Welcome aboard your journey to Spanish fluency! I'm so glad you're joining the ever-growing family of people who are curious and passionate about this amazing language. Have you always wanted to learn Spanish? Or just caught the bug recently? Either way, you're in the right place. Spanish is an incredible language in so many different ways, and mastering it will give you the keys to a wonderful culture with deep roots and remarkable history.

More than 430 million people worldwide speak Spanish as their native language. That makes it the second-largest native language in the world behind Mandarin (and before English!), and the fourth-most spoken language overall (trailing only Mandarin, English and Hindi).

Way beyond Europe, dozens of countries count Spanish as their official language. It's by far the most widespread language in the Americas – sharing the limelight only with English in North America,and Portuguese in Brazil – and it's also present in Asia and Africa. In fact, there are ten times more people speaking Spanish around the world than there are people in Spain! Crazy, right? So, needless to say, if you speak Spanish you vastly improve your chances of being understood no matter where you are.

A Fascinating History

Spanish is a lot more than numbers and figures. It's an immensely rich culture spanning across all continents. Spanish history is one of the grandest tales of human civilization. If you were to write a history of the modern world, you'd certainly grant it a major leading role. For centuries, Spain and Portugal were at the vanguard of global exploration, competing for shipping routes across the oceans and effectively giving birth to modern global trade. It played a central role in the religious struggles of the Middle Ages, created one of the largest and most powerful empires ever assembled, and emerged as the world's first global superpower.

Spanish is, therefore, an immensely interesting language, deeply grounded in history but also hugely relevant to modern times.

A Traveler's Best Friend

Your recent travels probably exposed you to overcrowded city centers and famous landmarks transformed into stale, money-making amusement parks. What's more insipid than checking monuments off a list for a weekend, surrounded by souvenir shops and restaurant chains? If you're someone yearning for cultural immersion, traveling like that just doesn't cut it.

Speaking the local language has an amazing impact on your adventures abroad. Whether in Madrid, Granada, Buenos Aires or Manilla, speaking Spanish will, therefore, allow you to separate yourself from the crowd and experience places the way they're supposed to be.

Thanks to your Spanish skills, you'll avoid the constant flow of noisy, obnoxious (and sometimes badly-behaved) tourists, and venture into local, non-commercial, residential areas. There, you'll be more likely to find what Spanish cities truly have to offer: their customs, traditions, and perhaps more importantly, their people.

Earning respect and friendship of local populations will add a wonderful dimension to your travels and unlock a coveted treasure: human interaction. Your willingness to approach locals in their own language will be appreciated as a mark of respect. You'll find people more inclined to talk to you, help you, and even befriend you.

And with Learn Like A Native, you'll have lots of fun along the way!

A Useful Business Tool

First impressions go a long way. In your search for a job, knowing other languages is a huge advantage that will separate you from the rest of the field. Employers will take your desire and ability to master another language as evidence of your willingness to try new things and see the world from a different perspective. Not only will Spanish look good on your CV, but it will also highlight your confidence to take on new challenges – a great trait for any potential employee.

Imagine now that your company's biggest client is a Spanish investor, an Argentinian businessman, or a Hispanic American banker. How impressed will your boss be to see you close a huge contract by befriending him through your exquisite Spanish skills? I'd say there's a good chance that your name will come up for the next promotion.

Imagine you discover a huge opportunity in the California market, and your contact point is a warm but tough Hispanic man with many options. A friendly relationship with a fellow Spanish-speaker could be the determining factor in his decision to do business with you rather than with someone else. In other words, don't underestimate the power of human contact. Especially in today's globalized world, adding Spanish to your business arsenal is a great way to get ahead of the pack, put yourself in favorable situations and create opportunities that just wouldn't exist otherwise.

The Perfect Method

I'm sure you've been told there's no right or wrong way to learn a language. Well, that can't be right, because it's wrong! The truth is, most people don't lack in motivation, drive, excitement, determination, or even talent. More than anything, people lack the correct method.

I've been learning and teaching languages my whole life, and I've realized that the number one reason why people get stuck learning any language is simple. It's not because they are lazy, it's not because they don't have time, it's because they are bored!

You could go to the best schools and have the best teachers in the world, but if you're bored in your Spanish class, you're unlikely to get anywhere. Starting from scratch and ingesting new knowledge and can be a daunting thing as it is. So, if you're not fully engaged, learning a new language will be a long road.

Think about it. You've been a child before. Did you learn grammar before you knew how to speak? Of course not! So why do that now? In my opinion, that's where most language methods fail. Because they get caught up in all the specific rules and formal details a language holds, before worrying about whether or not their students understand what's going on. What's the point in knowing irregular verbs, if you can't even order food at the restaurant! My point being, unless you're planning to write a Ph.D. in Spanish, the most important thing for you is to be able to speak with other people.

That's where Learn Like A Native comes in!

With approximately 90 million people who speak and study Spanish as a non-native language, there's plenty of opinions as to what the best way to learn is.

That's why I based my method on modern expert research. The latest studies show that the most efficient way to learn languages – and Spanish in particular – is by learning vocabulary and grammar in conversation.

Using this method, I'll teach you how to apply formal knowledge in a real-life environment, through practical and relatable materials. With short and fun lessons, you'll stay engaged every step of the way, helping you retain vocabulary much more efficiently.

The audiobook version is narrated by a Spanish native speaker who will get you comfortable with the sounds of the language. You'll take an active part in the learning process and be required to speak, repeat and exercise new sounds as they come up throughout the lessons.

Don't simply listen passively, but instead learn actively by practicing tough sounds such as the double "r," like a true native Spanish-speaker. If you have any trouble, the textbook will help you with written sounds so you can visualize letters and the sound they relate to.

www.LearnLikeNatives.com

You'll feel like you're in a Spanish class. But one you can take everywhere! With only 20 to 30 minutes per lesson, you can focus on each topic independently without any stress. Squeeze them into your schedule, sitting in your car or waiting for the Bus, and enjoy the flexibility of going through each step at your own pace. No one is watching you, of course, but I trust you'll do the work! Before you know it, you'll find yourself having a full-blown conversation in Spanish and wonder how you got there!

It's fun, easy-to-use, and most importantly, it works!

www.LearnLikeNatives.com

www.LearnLikeNatives.com

FREE BOOK!

Get the *FREE BOOK* that reveals the secrets path to learn any language fast, and without leaving your country.

Discover:

- The **language 5 golden rules** to master languages at will

- Proven **mind training techniques** to revolutionize your learning

- A complete step-by-step guide to **conquering any language**

www.LearnLikeNatives.com

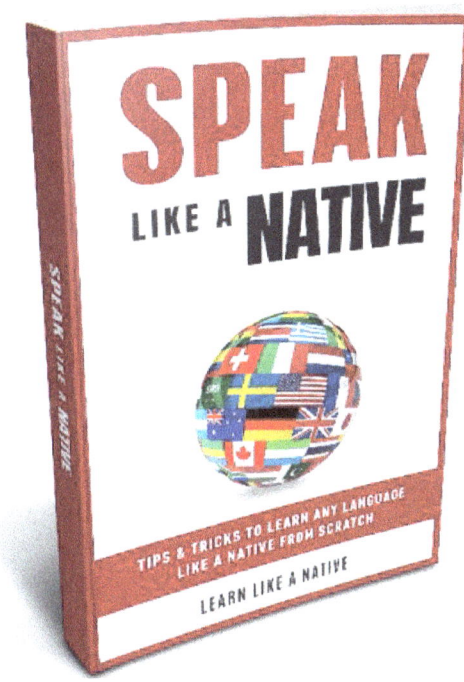

www.LearnLikeNatives.com

Chapter 1 – Dreaming of the South

You are sitting at home, thinking about vacation, and suddenly a friend calls you to tell you about their latest family travel to exotic South America--it was a beautiful, sunny, diverse, and entertaining place. You hang up and start imagining yourself with a Cuban mojito in hand, the sea in front of you.

Can you imagine kayaking with your family through the great blue sea of the Caribbean? Can you feel the hand of your loved one, the touch, while enjoying a glass of wine by the sunset? Just stay with me, because you can have it all.

To make this a reality, the first thing you need to search for are requirements, hotels, and transportation.

English	Spanish
To travel	Viajar
I want **to travel** to Cartagena.	Quiero **viajar** a Cartagena.

Vee-ah-har

Notice the "j" sound. For the Spanish language, "j" works the same way "h" does in English whenever preceding a vowel. For example, the word "house".

Now repeat: vee-ah-har.

Requirements	Requerimientos
Requirements to travel to Colombia.	**Requerimientos** para viajar a Colombia.

www.LearnLikeNatives.com

This is a typical "difficult" word for English speakers because Spanish has a different "r" sound. It has two different sounds: one for the "single r," and one for the "double r". We will not be too strict about this because it is mostly about practice. In any case, this is what I would recommend for pronunciation:

1. Lift your tongue and touch your hard palate with it. This is the space situated just behind your incisive upper teeth.

2. Breathe in and out through your mouth. This should make your tongue move at least a bit.

3. Repeat.

4. You can practice this until your "r" sounds like a kitten purring. Once you have achieved this, you can be confident you are getting it.

Back to requirements--checking this is very important: due to political and health challenges in many countries, it is possible that you may need some extra requirements to visit, such as vaccines or a travel visa.

Visa	Visa

Do I need a **visa** to travel to Colombia?	¿Necesito una **visa** para viajar a Colombia?

Please notice how the word "visa" is the same in both languages, as well as its pronunciation.

Next phrase.

Vaccines	Vacunas
Vaccines are needed to visit Colombia.	**Vacunas** necesarias para visitar Colombia.

"Vaccines" translates as "vacunas". This word can be split into three syllables: va-coo-nahs.

In case you have these requirements covered, the next step would be to look for flights.

Most airline platforms are multilingual. However, it is known that some domestic flights could be cheaper when bought with a national airline.

Airlines	Aerolíneas
What **airlines** travel to Cartagena?	¿Qué **aerolíneas** viajan a Cartagena?

This is a long and possibly difficult word, specifically because you need to use that single "r" sound. The sound difference between a single and a double will be given by the amount of air you breathe out. So, let's practice.

Ah-eh-ro-lí-neas

Something to keep in mind is that vowels in Spanish are very open and clear. For example, a Spanish "e" always has a similar sound as the one you would use to say "essay". That starting "e" sound is what we are looking for.

Flights	Vuelos
Find **flights** from Bogota to Cartagena.	Encontrar **vuelos** desde Bogotá hacia Cartagena.

You can notice how the word "from" translates to "desde", which is your starting point. While your destination is covered by "hacia".

One-way trip	Viaje de ida
Do you want a **one-way trip**?	¿Quieres un **viaje de ida**?

Round trip	Viaje de ida y vuelta

No, I want a **round trip**.	No. Quiero un **viaje de ida y vuelta**.

Dates	Fechas
Dates for your travel?	**¿Fechas** en las que viaja?

Repeat after me: Feh-chas

When looking for accommodations, you have many great references at your disposal, but it is always preferable to ask the locals for specifics related to the best and most touristy locations.

To stay	Alojarse
Best places **to stay** in Cartagena.	Mejores zonas para **alojarse** en Cartagena.

Touristic	Turísticas
Most **touristic** places in Cartagena.	Zonas más **turísticas** de Cartagena.

Once you have found somewhere you like, the next step is to book a room.

To Book	Reservar
I want to **book** a room.	Quiero **reservar** una habitación.

As you can see, this is another word where you need to put your double "r" into training. Repeat after me: reh-ser-var.

Good! Are we acing those r's or what?

Depending on how many people you include in your trip, you could choose a single room or a double room.

Single room	Habitación simple
I want a **single room**.	Quiero una **habitación simple**.

Double room	Habitación doble
I want a **double room**.	Quiero una **habitación doble**.

If you do not enjoy flying, perhaps other transportation methods could be useful.

Cruise	Crucero

| I want a **cruise** through the Caribbean. | Quiero un **crucero** por el Caribe. |

Crew-ce-ro

How do you feel so far? Ready to book a trip?

Great! Because now we are going to do some packing.

First, the verb that makes it happen: to pack.

| To pack | Empacar |
| I need to **pack** my baggage. | Necesito **empacar** mi equipaje. |

This is a double: you have "packing" and "baggage". These translate respectively as "empacar" and "equipaje".

With this in mind, repeat again: Necesito empacar mi equipaje.

Of course, you need a suitcase.

Suitcase	Maleta
I need a bigger **suitcase**.	Necesito una **maleta** más grande.

The word "maleta" can be used in general. However, similar to English, Spanish distinguishes a difference between your checked bags and your carry-on.

Checked bag	Maleta registrada
Your ticket includes one **checked bag**.	Tu boleto incluye una **maleta registrada**.

Carry-on	Equipaje de mano

Your **carry-on** is too big.	Tu **equipaje de mano** es muy grande.

With your suitcase on top of your bed, because that is how most of us do it, you are ready to start putting items inside.

Shirt	Camisa
I like this **shirt** for the trip.	Me gusta esta **camisa** para el viaje.

T-shirt	Camiseta
Why don't you bring a **t-shirt**? Something more sporty.	¿Por qué no empacas una **camiseta**? Algo más deportivo.

Pants	Pantalones
Should I bring some **pants**?	¿Debería llevar **pantalones**?

Shorts	Pantalones cortos
Maybe I should pack some **shorts**.	Tal vez debería empacar unos **pantalones cortos**.

Due to globalization, "shorts" is a common way to call short pants, even in Spanish speaking countries. Just in case, you have the neutral Spanish way.

Skirt/Dress	Falda/Vestido

I think I will pack a **skirt** and maybe a **dress**.	Creo que empacaré una **falda** y tal vez un **vestido**.

Skirt: fal-dah

Dress: ves-tee-doh

Sweater	Abrigo
I will bring a **sweater**.	Voy a empacar un **abrigo**.

This is a very useful one, so repeat: a-bree-goh. This is a word that can be used for "coat", from a sweater to a raincoat, and even shelter. Keep it in mind: "abrigo" will keep you warm if needed.

Underwear	Ropa interior
Pack **underwear** for a week.	Empaca **ropa interior** para una semana.

Socks	Calcetines
How many **socks** should I bring?	¿Cuántos **calcetines** debería llevar?

And, because we are already on it, it is a good idea to go through some body parts.

Feet	Pies
You have very cold **feet**.	Tienes los **pies** muy fríos.

Legs	Piernas

I have to shave my **legs**.	Tengo que rasurarme las **piernas**.

Hands	Manos
Do not forget the **hand** cream.	No olvides la crema de **manos**.
Arms	Brazos
I want to tan my **arms**.	Quiero broncearme los **brazos**.

Head	Cabeza

I got a bump on my **head**.	Tengo un chichón en la **cabeza**.

Face	Rostro
I need a **face** towel.	Necesito una toalla de **rostro**.

How are you doing so far? Are there any words you need to repeat?

After this short walkthrough of your body parts, I think we are ready to practice our first lesson. Shall we?

For this situation, we have prepared a call between you and a travel agent.

Agent: *Good afternoon! Where do you want to travel?*

¡Buenas tardes! ¿A dónde le gustaría viajar?

Allen: *Cartagena, Colombia.*

Cartagena, Colombia.

Agent: *Date for your travel?*

¿Fecha en la que viaja?

Allen: *December, 15th.*

15 de Diciembre.

Agent: *How many adults are traveling?*

¿Cuántos adultos viajan?

Allen: *Two, please.*

Dos, por favor.

Agent: *Are you traveling with kids?*

¿Viaja con niños?

Allen: *Yes. Two kids.*

Sí. Dos niños.

Agent: *Would you like a one-way trip or a round trip?*

¿Desea un viaje de ida, o un viaje de ida y vuelta?

Allen: *Round trip. Thank you.*

Viaje de ida y vuelta. Gracias.

Agent: *When do you wish to come back?*

¿Cuál fecha le gustaría para su regreso?

Allen: *January, 2nd.*

2 de enero.

Agent: *Okay. Our lowest fare is $350 per person, but it does not include checked bags. Would you like to add checked bags?*

Muy bien. Nuestra tarifa más baja es de $350 por persona, pero no incluye equipaje registrado. ¿Le gustaría añadir maletas registradas?

Allen: *Not at the moment. Thank you.*

No por el momento. Gracias.

Agent: *Very well. Would you like to book accommodations?*

Muy bien. ¿Le gustaría reservar alojamiento?

Allen: *Sure. What do you have?*

¡Claro! ¿Qué me ofreces?

Agent: *I can offer you two bedrooms. One double with a King size bed, and another double with two single beds.*

Puedo ofrecerle dos habitaciones. Una doble con una cama King, y otra habitación doble con dos camas individuales.

Allen: *Great!*

¡Genial!

Agent: *Perfect. Please, wait in line for a second so I can write down your details.*

Perfecto. Por favor, espere en línea para anotar sus datos.

How was this for you? Are you feeling more confident now? I hope you do, because we are about to take a flight.

Chapter 2 – Not Only Birds Can Fly

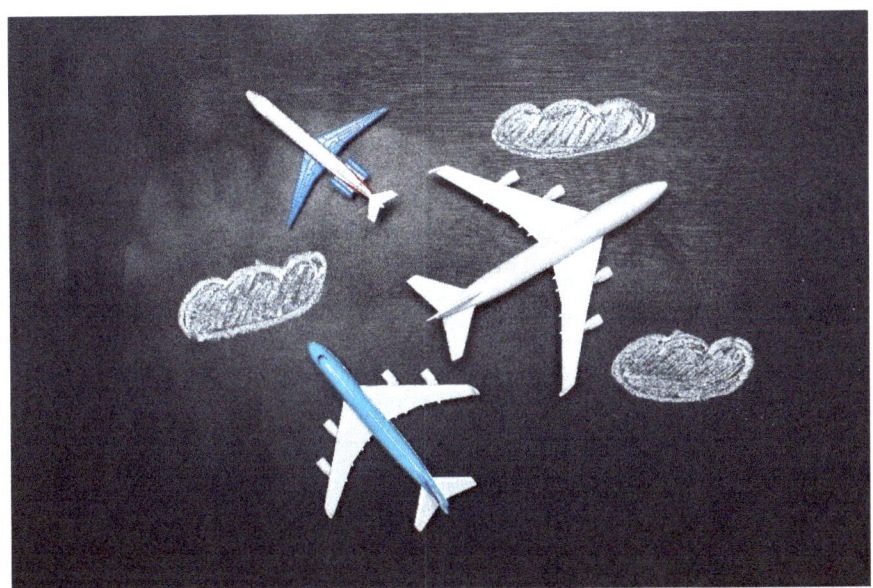

In my experience, airports can be stressful places for multiple reasons. They are crowded spaces with many lines to wait in and documents to show, and you have to do it every single time. Thankfully, I am here to help you be at your gate in time, stress-free.

Let's start by checking you in to your flight.

Passport	Pasaporte

| Can I please have your **passport**? | ¿Puedo ver su **pasaporte**? |

Pah-sah-por-teh

Being by the counter, it is a perfect time to practice what we learned in lesson one. They will ask you where you are traveling, how many people are traveling in your family group, and the number of bags you have. Overweight luggage is a VERY common topic of discussion.

| Overweight | Sobrepeso |
| This piece of luggage is **overweight**. | Esta pieza de equipaje tiene **sobrepeso**. |

Come again: so-bre-pe-so

If you skipped the overweight experience—which I hope, because those fees are usually very high—you are ready to go through TSA.

Tray	Bandeja
Please take off shoes, coats, and metal objects, and put your belongings in a **tray.**	Por favor, retirar zapatos, abrigos y objetos de metal, y colocar sus pertenencias en una **bandeja.**

Remember what we learned in lesson one about the Spanish "j"? Time to practice that "ha" sound.

Ban-deh-ha

Screen	Revisión
Please, go to the left for a second **screen.**	Por favor, diríjase a la izquierda para una segunda **revisión**.

Re-vee-seeon

Once you are in, it is time to look for your gate.

www.LearnLikeNatives.com

Gate	Puerta
Where is **gate** 15?	¿Dónde está la **puerta** 15?

Poo-air-tah

Flight	Vuelo
What **flight** are you taking?	¿Cuál **vuelo** vas a tomar?

Voo-eh-loh.

Boarding pass	Pase de abordar
Please, have your **boarding pass** and passport in hand.	Por favor, tenga su **pase de abordar** y pasaporte a la mano.

This is a tricky one because it is a compound word. So, let's take it slow.

Pah-se-the-ah-bor-thar

Seat	Asiento
My **seat** is 23F.	Mi **asiento** es el 23F.

Ah-see-N-toh

Bathroom	Baño
Is that **bathroom** occupied?	¿El **baño** está ocupado?

Bah-nio

Blanket	Cobija
Can I have a **blanket**?	¿Me puede dar una **cobija**?

Koh-bee-ha

You know. I could teach you how to ask for other stuff... like some wine? Which is vee-noh (repeat with me: vee-noh), but let's be responsible and learn some emergency signals.

Go through	Pasar
I need to **go through**.	Necesito **pasar**.

Pah-sar

Feeling sick	Sentirse enfermo
I am feeling **sick**.	Me siento **enfermo**.

N-fur-moh

"Sick" translates directly as "enfermo". So, work on your phrasing, but especially remember that word, "N-fur-moh". Hearing "sick" in any language is a sign for help.

Headache	Dolor de cabeza
I have a **headache**.	Tengo **dolor de cabeza**.

Doh-lorh-the-ka-beh-sa.

Fever	Fiebre
I have a **fever**.	Tengo **fiebre**.

Fee-e-bre

Nausea	Náusea
I feel **nauseous.**	Siento **náuseas**.

Nah-ooh-ce-us

Allergic	Alérgico

| I am **allergic** to... | Soy **alérgico** a... |

Ah-ler-hee-koh

Needless to say, I hope you will not need any of this emergency speech, but we are here to be prepared for whatever comes our way.

How are you feeling so far? Think of the things we have just learned. You can now go into an airport, get into a plane, enjoy a movie, and land safely. Join me for a little practice.

Flight Attendant: *Hello! Boarding pass, please.*

¡Hola! Pase de abordar, por favor.

Cris: *Hello!*

¡Hola!

Flight Attendant: *Welcome! You're at seat 14F. By the window.*

¡Bienvenida! Su asiento es el 14F. Junto a la ventana.

Cris: *Thanks!*

¡Gracias!

Flight Attendant:	*What would you like to drink today?*
	¿Qué le gustaría tomar hoy?
Cris:	*I would like some water with ice.*
	Quisiera un poco de agua con hielo.
Flight Attendant:	*Of course! Anything else I can do for you?*
	¡Por supuesto! ¿Algo más que pueda hacer por usted?
Cris:	*Yes, I am actually feeling a little sick.*
	Sí. En verdad me siento un poco enferma.
Flight Attendant:	*What are your symptoms?*
	¿Cuáles son sus síntomas?
Cris:	*I have a headache and a slight fever.*
	Tengo dolor de cabeza y un poco de fiebre.
Flight Attendant:	*Are you allergic to something?*
	¿Es alérgica a algo?
Cris:	*Only to aspirin.*
	Solo a la aspirina.

Flight Attendant:	*Ok. Please let me get help.*
	Está bien. Por favor, permítame buscar ayuda.

Yes, I know. I picked the sick-person-talk for this practice. Can you blame me? I told you I made this book to be sure you would be completely prepared! Is your head better? No? Don't worry. We are landing now.

www.LearnLikeNatives.com

Chapter 3 – Looking for a Ride?

Welcome to your dream vacation! Only one thing stands between you and a strawberry daiquiri by the pool: you have to get to your hotel. This is how you really test your knowledge. Being already at your destination means your super-intensive-Spanish-camp is about to start. How fun is that?

First, let's begin with some basic words.

Taxi	Taxi
I need a **taxi**.	Necesito un **taxi**.

Same word? 1 point for globalization!

Shuttle	Transporte
Where can I get a **shuttle** to the Hilton Cartagena?	¿Dónde puedo tomar el **transporte** para el Hilton Cartagena?

Trans-poor-teh

"Transporte" is one of those basic and general words you will want to have on your menu. Anything from a cab to a rented car is a transportation method and is, therefore, a "transporte". Repeat with me: "trans-poor-teh".

Bus	Autobús
Where can I take a **bus** downtown?	¿Dónde puedo tomar un **autobús** al centro?

Please, remember the sound for a Spanish "u" is like an English "oo". Other than that, this should be an easy one.

Au-to-boos

If you are traveling with family, you are possibly thinking about driving around. We should take you to a car rental.

Rent a car	Alquilar un auto
I want to **rent a car**.	Quiero **alquilar un auto**.

Al-kee-lar un au-toh

To nail a Spanish "t" sound, it's always good to think of a British one. A strong, clear "t" that you can feel on the tip of your tongue.

Driver's license	Licencia de conducir
I will need a **driver's license**.	Voy a necesitar una **licencia de conducir**.

Li-sen-sia the con-doo-sir

You have finally arrived at your hotel. The landscape is beautiful and bright, decorated by the sound of palm trees blowing in the wind. Can you feel it? Great! I can too! But you got to get settled first. We are almost there.

Check in	Registrarme
I would like to **check into** my room.	Quisiera **registrarme** en mi habitación.

Have you been practicing your double "r"? I hope you have! Go with me:

Rre-his-trar-meh

Reservation	Reservación
Under whose name is the reservation?	¿A nombre de quién está la **reservación?**

Key	Llave

| Here is your **key**. | Aquí está su **llave**. |

Yah-veh

This is going to depend on what type of hotel you stay in. They now have keycards (tarjetas), or you can even access by pin code (código). Again, basic general words will save your life.

Elevator	Ascensor
Elevator is down the hall.	El **ascensor** se encuentra al final del pasillo.

Floor	Piso
Our room is on the 7th **floor**.	Nuestra habitación está en el 7mo **piso**.

This one sounds like "pee-soh".

Hey! I know you are eager to go into your room, so let's get in.

Look around your bedroom. You will find a bed, maybe a flat-screen, and a closet. You can see the sunset coming through your window behind some light shades. Let's make some necessary introductions.

Bed	Cama
Honey! Our **bed** is huge!	¡Cariño! Nuestra **cama** es enorme.

Kah-mah

TV	Televisor
Is it a smart **TV**?	¿Es un **televisor** inteligente?

The-le-vee-sor

Closet	Armario
I'll put the suitcases inside the **closet**.	Pondré las maletas dentro del **armario**.

Ar-mah-reeo

At this point, you should be truly acing those purring sounds. Go inside your bathroom. Tubs are not so common in the tropics, but you will definitely have a shower and a toilet. Given that bathrooms go with water, and water leaks, you want to pay attention to the following words and phrases in case you have to report any problems with the pipes.

Shower	Ducha
We have a massage **shower**.	Tenemos una **ducha** de masaje.

Doo-cha. I know what you are thinking, this sounds like another word I know. Keep in mind that in Spanish, the "ch" sound is similar to the "sh" one, but stronger--more to the tip of the tongue.

Toilet	Inodoro
Two bathrooms! We have a **toilet** each.	¡Dos baños! Cada uno tiene un **inodoro**.

Ee-no-tho-ro

Sink	Lavabo
I will put some things by the **sink**.	Voy a poner algunas cosas cerca del **lavabo**.

La-va-boh

Towels	Toalla
Hello! I need more **towels**.	¡Hola! Necesito más **toallas**.

Pillows	Almohadas
I also need 2 more **pillows**.	También necesito 2 **almohadas** más.

Practice these last two with me:

Toh-ah-yas

Al-moh-ah-das

It turns out my girlfriend uses four pillows and I always use extra towels. These two are basic survival for us.

Also, some hotels don't put mini-fridges inside the bedrooms anymore. In case you have any requests, follow me to the next phrase.

Mini fridge	Mini refrigerador
I would like a **mini-fridge** in my bedroom.	Me gustaría tener un **mini-refrigerador** en mi habitación.

You know the word for "mini". Let's practice the hard one:
Rre-fri-he-ra-dor
Mini-refrigerador

You have a nice bedroom in there! So, how about some practice?

Concierge: Hello! How can I help you?

¡Hola! ¿Cómo puedo ayudarle?

Dan: Hello! I think my sink is leaking.

¡Hola! Creo que mi lavamanos está goteando.

Concierge: I will send someone right away!

¡Enviaré a alguien enseguida!

Dan: Thanks. I appreciate your help.

Gracias. Aprecio tu ayuda.

Concierge: I am sorry for the inconvenience. Is there anything I can do to make your stay more pleasant?

Siento mucho los inconvenientes. ¿Hay algo que pueda hacer para que su estadía sea más placentera?

Dan: *Now that you mention it, I notice my room does not have a mini-fridge.*

Ahora que lo mencionas, noté que mi habitación no tiene mini-refrigerador.

Concierge: *Of course! Anything else?*

¡Claro! ¿Algo más?

Dan: *I'd like a couple more towels, and one extra pillow, please.*

Quisiera un par de toallas más, y una almohada extra, por favor.

Concierge: *Sure! Just in case you need more pillows, you have an extra inside the closet.*

¡Por supuesto! En caso de que necesitara más almohadas, hay una extra dentro del armario.

Dan: *Good to know! Thanks!*

¡Es bueno saberlo! ¡Gracias!

Concierge: *Is there anything else I can do for you today?*

¿Hay algo más que pueda hacer por usted el día de hoy?

Dan: *I am okay. Thank you very much.*

Estoy bien. Muchas gracias.

Concierge: *I will send help right away. Again, sorry for the inconvenience.*

Enviaré ayuda de inmediato. Nuevamente, me disculpo por los inconvenientes.

Dan: *It is all good. Thanks for your help.*

Está bien. Gracias por tu ayuda.

Concierge: *Thank you for being our guest!*

Gracias a usted por ser nuestro huésped.

Good! I think we are all set! Ready to go work on your tan?

Chapter 4 – I Find My Happiness Where the Sun Shines

You are finally here, in your dreamland. It is warm, and the sound of the ocean follows you all the way to your room. Far away, you hear some drums playing. This is all you wanted, and now you are ready to enjoy it. Aren't you? Let's check the weather for a second.

Weather	Clima

How's the **weather** in Colombia?	Cómo es el **clima** en Colombia?

First, just a quick check-up on the seasons.

Spring	Primavera
Flowers are blooming. **Spring** is here.	Las flores están floreciendo. Ha llegado la **primavera.**

Pree-ma-veh-ra

Summer	Verano
In the tropics, it always feels like **summer**.	En el trópico, siempre se siente como **verano**.

Be-rah-noh

Again, remember to work on your "open" vowels. The clearer, the better.

Fall	Otoño
Look at the trees, and their **fall** colors.	Mira los árboles y sus colores de **otoño**.

Oh-to-nio

As you know, the weather can surprise us. We know summer is supposed to be hot, and winter is cold, but so many other factors can add to it. Let's check some.

Cloud	Nube
Look at that big **cloud**.	Mira esa gran **nube.**

Noo-beh

Sun	Sol
The **sun** was too strong.	El **sol** estaba muy fuerte.

Rain	Lluvia
The **rain** came without a warning.	La **lluvia** vino sin avisar.

Yiu-veeah

Storm	Tormenta
Before we knew, the **storm** was here.	Antes de que supiéramos, la **tormenta** estaba aquí.

Thor-men-ta

Are any popular characters coming to mind? I bet there are!

Wind	Viento
The **wind** was so strong that the windows were moving.	El **viento** era tan fuerte que las ventanas se estaban moviendo.

Degrees	Grados
We were under 0 **degrees**.	Estábamos por debajo de 0 **grados**.

Grah-dos

Something to keep in mind is that the metric system is common outside the US. Depending on your destination, having a unit converter could be very useful.

Hurricane	Huracán

The **hurricane** wrecked it all.	El **huracán** lo destruyó todo.

Ooh-rah-can. It's the perfect word to practice your single "r" soft sound with.

Sunglasses	Lentes de sol
I left my **sunglasses** on the bed!	¡Dejé mis **lentes de sol** sobre la cama!

Lin-tes-the-sol

Hat	Sombrero
That's a nice **hat**!	¡Ese es un buen **sombrero**!

Som-breh-roh

www.LearnLikeNatives.com

This is a word many English speakers are used to hearing, which is great. Sombrero could generally stand for any kind of hat, including caps.

Sunscreen	Protector solar
Did you bring **sunscreen**?	Trajiste **protector solar**?

Pro-tek-tor so-lar

Umbrella	Sombrilla
Let's get under that **umbrella**.	Vamos a ponernos bajo esa **sombrilla**.

Sun-bree-ya

Raincoat	Impermeable

| It is necessary to bring your **raincoat.** | Es necesario traer su **impermeable**. |

In-per-meh-ah-bleh

This is a good word. "Impermeable" is the Spanish word for waterproof, so it is something to keep in mind when you go shopping.

Talking about shopping, why don't we go for a little spree?

Seller: *Hello! Good afternoon. How can I help you?*

¡Hola! Buenas tardes. ¿Cómo puedo ayudarle?

Ken: *Hey! Good afternoon. I would like to buy some things.*

¡Hola! Buenas tardes. Me gustaría comprar algunas cosas.

Seller: *Sure! What do you have in mind?*

¡Seguro! ¿Qué tiene en mente?

Ken: *Everything. I need an umbrella, sunglasses, a raincoat... everything.*

	Todo. Necesito una sombrilla, lentes de sol, un impermeable… todo.
Seller:	*Oh, I see. Did the hurricane catch you off guard?*
	Oh, ya veo. ¿El huracán le tomó por sorpresa?
Ken:	*Yes. Totally. It's been crazy. Sun goes and rain comes. Repeatedly.*
	Sí. Totalmente. Ha sido una locura. El sol se va y viene la lluvia. Repetidamente
Seller:	*I am sorry to hear that. I will help you, gladly.*
	Siento escuchar eso. Le ayudaré, con mucho gusto.
Ken:	*Thanks! What raincoats do you have?*
	¡Gracias! ¿Cuáles impermeables tienes?
Seller:	*I have these raincoats. Good quality and they protect you down to 0 degrees.*
	Tengo estos impermeables. Buena calidad y le protege hasta los 0 grados.
Ken:	*Awesome! What about umbrellas?*
	¡Genial! ¿Cuáles sombrillas tienes?
Seller:	*I have many. It depends on what size you are looking for.*

Tengo muchas. Depende de qué tamaño busca.

Ken: *Just a couple of small umbrellas. Something easy to carry.*

Solo un par de sombrillas pequeñas. Algo que sea fácil de cargar.

Seller: *Sure! Why don't you come with me to pick sunglasses?*

¡Por supuesto! ¿Por qué no me acompaña a elegir lentes de sol?

Ken: *Glad to! I will follow you.*

¡Encantando! Te sigo.

Seller: *Very well. This way, please.*

Muy bien. Por acá, por favor.

I hope you have sunscreen. The rain is finally gone, so we are going to some touristy places in a while, and I do not want you to get a nasty sunburn. Remember to bring all of your equipment. As always, the most important thing is to be prepared.

Chapter 5 – I Have So Many Stories to Tell You

Do you know what I love most about life in general? The stories! And this is especially true for traveling because it is all about learning new cultures, meeting new and different people, and facing things you never thought you would.

I remember being in this beautiful colonial place in Queretaro, Mexico. Everything looked perfect. The location was terrific; it was close to all the tourist attractions, and the architecture in our hotel was breathtakingly beautiful. The price was good. Everything was perfect... until I got to my room and found my toilet was inside the shower.

Trust me. I am not picky. I decided to stay there for the night because the location was amazing and the hotel had already been paid for. I have to admit, though, that all optimism vanished after I went to the bathroom in the middle of the night and got my socks wet from the shower. Needless to say, it was a GREAT and funny story to tell my friends and one of those things I will remember forever.

If you are a storyteller, as I am, then you need a few more tools so you can delight your friends—even your newest local friends—with the fantastic things you have gone through. For that, we will use two different verbal forms to help you bring your story to life. You know this, or at least you may have heard of it back in school. Don't worry. We promised no grammar, okay? I want to show you some examples.

First, let's go through the first one: past simple, which in Spanish, we call "pretérito indefinido". It is close to "undefined past", something great for grammar and AWFUL for blind dates.

Regular verbs in Spanish can have 1 of 3 terminations: -ar (as in "viajar"), -er (as in "comer") and -ir (as in "descubrir"). This is important because, as you will see, once you can spot the termination of the verb, you will be able to figure out all conjugations without memorizing them.

For practical uses, we will group 3rd person pronouns as singular. "He", "she", and "it" will form a group.

We'll start with a verb we know: "viajar" – to travel.

To travel	Viajar	Root	Termination
I traveled	Yo viajé	Viaj-	Ar changes to "é"
You traveled	Tú viajaste		Ar changes to "aste"

He/She/It traveled	Él/Ella/Eso viajó		Ar changes to "ó"
We traveled	Nosotros viajamos		Ar changes to "amos"
You traveled	Ustedes viajaron		Ar changes to "aron"
They traveled	Ellos/Ellas viajaron		Ar changes to "aron"

Do you see what we did there? For conjugating regular verbs, you need to spot the root of the verb and then shift the termination, according to each case. For the verb "viajar", the root is "viaj-". For the verb "gustar" (to like), the root is "gust-". And for the verb "formar" (to form), we have to employ the root "form-".

The same thing will happen for the group of verbs ending in "er", as in "comer" (root "com-") or "sorprender" (root "sorprend-"), and for the "ir" termination group, as in "hundir" (root "hund-") or "compartir" (root "compart-").

Come on! It may look hard, but it is not really that awful. You just need some practice and a few pointers, like the ones we discussed.

Let's go for a quick practice.

I traveled to Spain last year.	Yo viajé a España el año pasado.
She traveled through the entire continent.	Ella viajó a través de todo el continente.
You traveled a lot the last two months.	Ustedes viajaron bastante los últimos dos meses.
We traveled to Mexico during the summer.	Nosotros viajamos a México durante el verano.

Can you see it? In every sentence, all the actions have already happened: last year, last summer, the last two months. Past perfect is for things in the past. Let's keep checking on this with the second termination, "er".

To eat	**Comer**	**Root**	**Termination**
I ate	Yo comí	Com-	Er changes to "í"

You ate	Tú comiste		Er changes to "iste"
He/She/It ate	Él/Ella/Eso comió		Er changes to "ió"
We ate	Nosotros comimos		Er changes to "imos"
You ate	Ustedes comieron		Er changes to "ieron"
They ate	Ellos/Ellas comieron		Er changes to "ieron"

Let's practice with some sentences.

You ate the entire cake.	Tú comiste todo el pastel.
She ate only a piece of cake.	Ella comió solo un pedazo de pastel.
We ate one piece each.	Nosotros comimos un pedazo cada uno.
They ate the rest of the cake.	Ellos comieron el resto del pastel.

www.LearnLikeNatives.com

This is important for stories—you have to eat. Also, as seen, it is a good verb to help solve some family culinary disputes.

To discover	Descubrir	Root	Termination
I discovered	Yo descubrí	Descubr-	Ir changes to "í"
You discovered	Tú descubriste		Ir changes to "íste"
He/She/It discovered	Él/Ella/Eso descubrió		Ir changes to "ió"
We discovered	Nosotros descubrimos		Ir changes to "imos"
You discovered	Ustedes descubrieron		Ir changes to "ieron"
They discovered	Ellos/Ellas descubrieron		Ir changes to "ieron"

Are you getting closer? Let's go for some practice.

You discovered a new way.	Tú descubriste una nueva manera.
He discovered his present.	Él descubrió su regalo.
You discovered a mark under the door.	Ustedes descubrieron una marca bajo la puerta.

They discovered that there was no door.	Ellos descubrieron que no había una puerta.

As we discussed earlier, for all regular verbs ending in "er", you only have to find the root and then add the termination for the conjugation you want.

How are you doing so far? Don't worry. We will keep working on this a little longer, using more examples.

Our next verb is "to have". "To have" and "to be" are fundamental in building complex sentences, but they are also on the list of irregular verbs for English and Spanish, so the changes we described earlier will not work for these verbs. Let's take a look.

To have	**Tener**
I had	Yo tuve
You had	Tú tuviste
He/She/It had	Él/Ella/Eso tuvo
We had	Nosotros tuvimos
You had	Ustedes tuvieron

| They had | Ellos/Ellas tuvieron |

Do you want to go for some practice?

I had such a great night. It was magical.	Yo tuve una gran noche. Fue mágica.
You had everything you asked for.	Tú tuviste todo lo que pediste.
She had a beautiful dress.	Ella tenía un hermoso vestido.
We had so much to be grateful.	Nosotros tuvimos mucho que agradecer.

The next verb is a little more complex and kind of philosophic—it is the verb "to be". For English, as well as for Spanish, it is the verb of existence. It turns out, in Spanish it translates to two different verbs: the verb "ser" and the verb "estar". Let's see how this works.

To be	**Ser**	**Estar**
I was	Yo fui	Yo estuve

You were	Tú fuiste	Tú estuviste
He/She/It was	Él/Ella/Eso fue	Él/Ella/Eso estuvo
We were	Nosotros fuimos	Nosotros estuvimos
You were	Ustedes fueron	Ustedes estuvieron
They were	Ellos/Ellas fueron	Ellos/Ellas estuvieron

You may be wondering: when should I use what?

The verb "ser" applies to the following cases:

- When defining or identifying someone or something. For example: "Ese fue Juan." – "That was Juan."; "Ustedes fueron soldados." – "You were soldiers."
- When describing someone's or something's characteristics. As in, "Tú fuiste muy hermosa." – "You were so beautiful." Or, "Ellos fueron muy rápidos." – "They were really quick."
- When speaking of the weather, the time of the day, and similar topics. "Eso fue en el otoño." – "It was in the autumn."; "Eso fue alrededor de las cuatro de la tarde." – "It was around four in the afternoon."

- When locating an event. "La fiesta fue en casa de Natalia." – "The party was at Natalia's house.; "La cumbre fue en San Francisco." – "The Summit was in San Francisco."

On the other side, the verb "estar" applies for these cases:

- When locating people and things in space. "Yo estuve en California." – "I was in California."; "Ellos estuvieron en la casa todo el tiempo." – "They were at home all the time."
- When speaking of someone's or something's state. "Ella estuvo sola todo el tiempo." – "She was alone all the time."; "Ellos estuvieron desordenados." – "They were messy."

First, a quick practice with the conjugations for "ser".

I was so happy that night.	Yo fui tan feliz aquella noche.
She was Prom Queen.	Ella fue Reina del Baile.
We were young once.	Nosotros fuimos jóvenes una vez.
They were invincible.	Ellos fueron invencibles.

Are you feeling good about this one? Let's go for "estar".

I was there all night.	Yo estuve ahí toda la noche.
He was busy that night.	Él estuvo ocupado esa noche.
We were by the pool.	Nosotros estuvimos junto a la piscina.
They were M.I.A.	Ellos estuvieron perdidos en acción.

As with any other language, Spanish is all about structure, and I promise it will get easier with some practice. As always, I will point other practical uses for this tense through the dialogue.

I said before, I was going to make a revision through two verbal forms. First was the undefined past. As you may have noticed, undefined past actions have already happened.

On the other side, in sentences using the imperfect past, you never know when the action started or ended. It's the equivalent to say that "you used to" do something. You know it's not happening anymore, but can't really tell when it ended. With this being said, let's see some examples using the same verbs as before.

To travel	Viajar	Root	Termination
I traveled	Yo viajaba	Viaj-	Ar changes to "aba"
You traveled	Tú viajabas		Ar changes to "abas"
He/She/It traveled	Él/Ella/Eso viajaba		Ar changes to "aba"
We traveled	Nosotros viajábamos		Ar changes to "ábamos"
You traveled	Ustedes viajaban		Ar changes to "aban"
They traveled	Ellos/Ellas viajaban		Ar changes to "aban"

Bee-ah-ha-ba; bee-ah-ha-bas; bee-ah-ha-bah-mos; bee-ah-ha-ban

I traveled all the time, until I lost my passport.	Yo viajaba todo el tiempo, hasta que perdí mi pasaporte.

She traveled the continent while he was getting his degree.	Ella viajaba el continente, mientras él estaba obteniendo su título.
You traveled before having kids.	Ustedes viajaban antes de tener a los niños.
We traveled every two months.	Nosotros viajábamos cada dos meses.

Notice how in these last sentences, you could have used "used to travel" instead of "traveled". This is important because it works as a hint—every time you can change an English verb in the past tense for a "used to + verb", you are in the presence of Spanish imperfect past, and therefore all changes apply as we just practiced.

I used to travel all the time until I lost my passport.	Yo viajaba todo el tiempo, hasta que perdí mi pasaporte.
She used to travel the continent, while he was getting his degree.	Ella viajaba el continente, mientras él estaba obteniendo su título.
You used to travel before having kids.	Ustedes viajaban antes de tener a los niños.

We used to travel every two months.	Nosotros viajábamos cada dos meses.

Are you getting better with your phrasing? Let's keep working.

To eat	Comer	Root	Termination
I ate	Yo comía	Com-	Er changes to "ía"
You ate	Tú comías		Er changes to "ías"
He/She/It ate	Él/Ella/Eso comía		Er changes to "ía"
We ate	Nosotros comíamos		Er changes to "íamos"
You ate	Ustedes comían		Er changes to "ían"
They ate	Ellos/Ellas comían		Er changes to "ían"

www.LearnLikeNatives.com

As always, don't worry. Practice makes perfect, and in no time, you will have each tense covered. Let's keep practicing.

You ate an entire cake while I was watching TV.	Tú comías un pastel mientras yo veía la televisión.
She ate one piece of cake after dinner every night.	Ella comía un pedazo de pastel luego de la cena, cada noche.
We ate one piece every time we saw each other.	Nosotros comíamos un pedazo, cada vez que nos veíamos.
That night, they ate with so much joy!	¡Esa noche, ellos comían con tanta alegría!

How is this sounding to you? Is it making any sense? Let's see more verbs.

To discover	Descubrir	Root	Termination
I discovered	Yo descubría	Descubr-	Ir changes to "ía"
You discovered	Tú descubrías		Ir changes to "ías"
He/She/It discovered	Él/Ella/Eso descubría		Ir changes to "ía"

We discovered	Nosotros descubríamos		Ir changes to "íamos"
You discovered	Ustedes descubrían		Ir changes to "ían"
They discovered	Ellos/ellas descubrían		Ir changes to "ían"

Can you see how the terminations shift? Let's see some examples.

I discovered new ways, before that happened.	Yo descubría nuevas formas, antes de que eso sucediera.
You discovered new ways to surprise me, night after night.	Tú descubrías nuevas formas de sorprenderme, noche tras noche.
She discovered a mark, and then another.	Ella descubría una marca, y luego otra.
They discovered what happened, until you found out.	Ellos descubrían qué sucedía, hasta que tú te enteraste.

See? It can get easier, quick. Let's go to our next verb: the irregular "to have", or "tener".

To have	Tener
I had	Yo tenía
You had	Tú tenías
He/She/It had	Él/Ella/Eso tenía
We had	Nosotros teníamos
You had	Ustedes tenían
They had	Ellos/Ellas tenían

Teh-nee-ah; teh-nee-us; teh-nee-ah-mos; teh-ní-an

I had everything I could wish.	Yo tenía todo lo que podía desear.
She had every opportunity.	Ella tenía todas las oportunidades.
You had other plans, and it worked.	Tú tenías otros planes, y funcionó.

We had so much to do.	Nosotros teníamos mucho por hacer.

Pay attention to the next verb. The verb "to be" is also an option when building sentences that are more complex. This turns it into a necessary tool to have in order to tell a great story.

To be	**Ser**	**Estar**
I was	Yo era	Yo estaba
You were	Tú eras	Tú estabas
He/She/It was	Él/Ella/Eso era	Él/Ella/Eso estaba
We were	Nosotros éramos	Nosotros estábamos
You were	Ustedes eran	Ustedes estaban
They were	Ellos/Ellas eran	Ellos/Ellas estaban

Es-tah-bah; es-tah-bas; es-tah-bah-mos; es-tah-ban

Let's practice a bit more.

I was a Prom Queen.	Yo era Reina del Baile.
He was a great athlete.	Él era un gran atleta.
We were a great team.	Nosotros éramos un gran equipo.
They were invincible.	Ellos eran invencibles.

Now that we have gone through the verbs "to have" and "to be" in the past tense, we can build on some more complex tenses.

We have the "pretérito anterior". First, let me give an example:

When it had finished raining, I kept walking.

As you can see, you combine "had" ("have" in the past tense) with another regular verb in past participle to indicate two actions that are finished with, one after the other.

In Spanish, that structure remains.

Cuando hubo terminado de llover, seguí caminando.

I understand you may be a little confused now. Do not rush. Let's see some more examples.

When he had awakened, she was already gone.	Cuando él hubo despertado, ella ya se había ido.
Once they had found the ball, they came back to play.	Cuando ellos hubieron encontrado la bola, volvieron a jugar.
As soon as I had studied, I took five minutes for myself.	Tan pronto hube estudiado, tomé cinco minutos para mí.

Through our dialogue, you will have the chance to see how all these elements fit together.

Kate: *Hello! I am so glad you came back from your trip.*

¡Hola! Estoy muy alegre de que hayas regresado de tu viaje.

Alex: *Hi! I am glad as well. It was a fun trip.*

¡Hola! Yo también estoy contento. Fue un viaje gracioso.

Kate: *Great! Tell me!*

¡Genial! Cuéntame.

Alex: *Remember how I used to love rain?*

¿Recuerdas cómo me encantaba la lluvia?

Kate: *Of course.*

Por supuesto.

Alex: *It turns out it was raining in Puebla, but I had bought tickets to see a movie.*

Resulta que estaba lloviendo en Puebla, pero había comprado boletos para ver una película.

Kate: *Such a pity!*

¡Que pena!

Alex: *I have always had that thing with rain.*

Siempre he tenido esa cosa con la lluvia.

Kate: *Indeed.*

Efectivamente.

Do you feel like an expert at putting phrases together? You should. We have come a long way. Besides, you are going to need those skills now because we are going on an adventure.

Chapter 6 – So Many Roads and So Many Places

I personally love to walk. Being younger, and single, I would put my earphones in and walk through any new city I got the chance to visit. When with my girlfriend, I put the earphones away and we enjoy long chats while walking and looking around. Sometimes she takes pictures, and they are mostly of me taking pictures of her, or the landscape. But I so enjoy watching her under all the diverse shades and lights. Have you ever noticed how every city has different colors and vibes?

Back to business. Tell me: what do you typically want to visit first when exploring a new city? Wherever you want to go, I am here to help you. Why don't we start with a few basics?

Museum	Museo
Where is the Prado **Museum**?	¿Dónde está el **Museo** del Prado?

Moo-se-oh

The first syllable is easy. Just think of the sound a cow makes, "moooo-seh-oh".

Square	Plaza
How can I get to Santo Domingo **Square**?	Cómo puedo llegar a la **Plaza** Santo Domingo?

Pla-za

Avenue	Avenida
What can I find on Alameda **avenue?**	¿Qué puedo encontrar en la **avenida** Alameda?

Ah-veh-nee-da

This one should not be a problem. The pronunciation is very similar to "avenue".

Monuments	Monumentos
Peru is rich in history and **monuments.**	Perú es rico en historia y **monumentos.**

Moh-noo-men-tos

Park	Parque
Park Güell is in Barcelona.	El **Parque** Güell está en Barcelona.

Par-ke

Church	Iglesia
They gave me this **church** as a reference.	Me dieron esta **iglesia** como referencia.

Ee-gle-si-a

Not to be unholy, but traveling is not just about history and great buildings. It is also about having fun and experiencing the true local culture, such as going to bars and clubs.

Bar	Bar
Where is this **bar**?	¿Dónde está ese **bar**?

See? Globalization scores again!

Now that you know some places, let's take you to them.

Across	Cruzando
You can find them **across** the avenue.	Puedes encontrarlos **cruzando** la avenida.

This should be a piece of cake. Say, "cruise" (like the boat) and add "ando" at the end.

In front of	Delante de
He is waiting **in front of** the statue.	Él está esperando **delante de** la estatua.

Deh-lant-te-de

Opposite	Opuesto
We were walking in the **opposite** direction.	Estábamos caminando en la dirección **opuesta.**

Oh-poo-es-tah

Street	Calle
You can find it down the **street.**	Puedes encontrarlo al final de la **calle.**

Ka-ye

Blocks	Cuadras
How many **blocks** are left?	¿Cuántas **cuadras** nos faltan?

Ku-ah-dras

Subway	Subterráneo
We can get there by **subway.**	Podemos llegar a través del **subterráneo.**

Ready for this one? Sub-te-rra-neo.

Mall	Centro comercial

| What kind of **mall** would you like to visit? | ¿Qué tipo de **centro comercial** te gustaría visitar? |

Cen-tro ko-mer-sial

Recommend	Recomendar
What can you **recommend?**	¿Qué me puedes **recomendar?**

Re-co-men-dar

"Recomendar" is a general word for "suggestions". So, whenever you are out of ideas, just remember this one.

In terms of tourism, you should already be an expert at getting around. You have learned how to request a cab, rent a car, and ask for directions and recommendations. You are almost done with this section, so why don't we practice a little more?

Front desk (Recepción): *Hello! How can I help you?*

¡Hola! ¿Cómo puedo ayudarle?

Allen: *I would like some recommendations for places to visit.*

	Me gustarían algunas recomendaciones de lugares para visitar.
Front desk:	*Very well. What type of place did you have in mind? A club, a museum?*
	Muy bien. ¿Qué clase de lugar tiene en mente? ¿Un club, un museo…?
Allen:	*I have heard that you have beautiful squares and monuments in this city.*
	He escuchado que tienen hermosas plazas y monumentos en esta ciudad.
Front desk:	*That is true. Sadly, most cultural attractions are across town.*
	Eso es cierto. Lamentablemente, la mayoría de las atracciones culturales está cruzando la ciudad.
Philip:	*Oh, I see. Could you give me some directions, please?*
	Oh, ya veo. ¿Podría darme algunas direcciones, por favor?
Front desk:	*Sure! Would you like to travel by car or take the subway?*
	¡Claro! ¿Le gustaría viajar en auto o tomar el subterráneo?

Philip: *I would rather take a subway and walk.*

Prefiero tomar el subterráneo y caminar.

Front desk: *Very well. The subway is only 3 blocks away.*

Muy bien. El subterráneo se encuentra a solo 3 cuadras.

Philip: *Perfect! How do I get there?*

¡Perfecto! ¿Cómo llego hasta allá?

Front desk: *You only have to go down this street, take a right, and walk straight for 3 blocks.*

Solo tiene que caminar hasta el final de la calle, doblar a la derecha y caminar recto durante 3 cuadras.

Philip: *That sounds easy. Thank you very much!*

Eso suena fácil. ¡Muchísimas gracias!

Front desk: *All right, then. After you get to the subway, go to the mainline and take a train to Baquedano station.*

Muy bien, entonces. Luego de llegar al subterráneo, vaya a la línea principal y tome un tren a la estación Baquedano.

Philip: *Very good. I appreciate your help.*

Muy bien. Aprecio su ayuda.

Front desk: *My pleasure. Have a nice day.*

Un placer. Que tenga un lindo día.

Allen: *Likewise. Bye.*

Igualmente. Adiós.

Ready to walk and get lost in new cities? I bet you are eager to do it. You better get dressed, go out, enjoy, and gather all the amazing stories you can!

I am feeling a little hungry, though. What do you say? Should we go and grab a bite?

www.LearnLikeNatives.com

Chapter 7 – Eat, Travel, Love

Food is one of my favorite parts of traveling. Eating is an awesome way to learn a bit more about the culture and history of each place. Your nose and tongue become guides that can lead you through unknown passages, allowing you to enjoy the aromas of Chile in a glass of cabernet; or the Mexican spice in a dish of mole poblano; or to experience the culinary revolution in Peru, in the shape of a sweet and sour mango ceviche. Flavors are unique everywhere you go, and that is what makes them a huge part of traveling.

For this reason, I want to be sure I am giving you the opportunity to have the best experience ever. Plus, ordering food is a recurrent activity, which means you will have many chances to practice. I can also assure you something: some of the best typical food places will not have a translator. With that in mind, let's start this chapter.

Restaurant	Restaurante
Let's go into that **restaurant.**	Vamos a entrar a ese **restaurante.**

Rehs-taoo-ran-teh

It is very similar to the English word, yet remember to put emphasis on the open vowels.

Table	Mesa
Table for 4, please.	**Mesa** para 4, por favor.

Meh-sa

Suggestions	Sugerencias
Do you want to hear today's **suggestions?**	¿Quieren escuchar las **sugerencias** de hoy?

Suh-he-ren-sias

Portion	Ración
I want a **portion** of fries.	Quiero una **ración** de papas fritas.

Rah-seeon

This is becoming easier with time, huh?

Fork	Tenedor
I dropped my **fork.**	Dejé caer mi **tenedor.**

Teh-neh-door

Spoon	Cuchara
Can I get a **spoon**?	Puedes darme una **cuchara**?

Cu-cha-ra

Do you remember this sound? Put it in the top of your tongue, so the "ch" will be stronger.

Knife	Cuchillo

I will need a meat **knife**.	Necesitaré un **cuchillo** para carnes.

Cu-chi-yo

Plate	Plato
Can you bring an extra **plate**?	¿Puedes traer un **plato** extra?

Appetizer	Entrada
Do you want an **appetizer**?	¿Quieres una **entrada**?

N-tra-da

"Entrada" is a good word because it translates both as an appetizer and as an entry. So, if ever looking for an entry, remember: "n-tra-da".

Main dish	Plato principal
For the **main dish**, I want the chicken.	Como **plato principal**, quiero el pollo.

Okay, we already practiced "plato" when learning "plate". "Plato" can mean both the instrument, as well as the actual food when speaking of a type of dish.

Pla-toh-preen-si-pal

Well-cooked	Bien cocido
I want my steak **well-cooked.**	Quiero mi bisteck **bien cocido.**

Bee-n ko-si-doh

Bee-n means "good".

Medium	Término medio
Medium is fine for me.	**Término medio** está bien para mí.

Tehr-mee-no-meh-dee-o

Dessert	Postre
Of course, I want a **dessert.**	Por supuesto, quiero un **postre.**

Pus-treh

Vegan	Vegano
Do you have a vegan menu?	¿Tiene menú **vegano**?

Beh-gah-no

Check	Cuenta
I want my **check**, please.	Quiero mi **cuenta**, por favor.

Quen-tah

Are you excited to order your first dish? Why don't we go to practice a bit more before…

Waiter (mesonero): *Good afternoon! Welcome to our restaurant. My name is Shawn. How many are you?*

¡Buenas tardes! Bienvenidos a nuestro restaurante. Mi nombre es Shawn. ¿Cuántos son ustedes?

Mike: *Hello! We have a reservation under Paulson. Table for 4.*

¡Hola! Tenemos una reservación a nombre de Paulson. Mesa para 4.

Waiter: *Yes, here you are. Come with me, please.*

Sí, aquí están. Vengan conmigo, por favor.

Mike: *I would like to order right away. We are starving.*

Quisiera ordenar de inmediato. Estamos muriendo de hambre.

Waiter: *Perfect. What would you like to order?*

Perfecto. ¿Qué desean ordenar?

Mike: *What are your suggestions?*

¿Cuáles son tus sugerencias?

Waiter: *The lobster ceviche as an appetizer. For the main dish, we have a causa accompanied by a saffron sauce.*

El ceviche de langosta como entrada. Como plato principal, tenemos una Causa acompañada de salsa de azafrán.

Mike: *Sounds great! I want one of each. Also, a salad and two beef dishes.*

¡Suena fabuloso! Quiero uno de cada uno. Además, quiero una ensalada y dos platos de carne.

Waiter:	*Do you want extra plates to share?*
	¿Quieren platos extra para compartir?
Mike:	*Yes, please.*
	Sí, por favor.
Waiter:	*Perfect. I will be back in a second with your plates, forks, and meat knives.*
	Perfecto. Volveré en un segundo con sus platos, tenedores y cuchillos de carne.
Mike:	*Thank you very much.*
	Muchas gracias.
Waiter:	*I'll be right back.*
	Volveré de inmediato.

I bet this chapter was easy. How did you feel after repeating that last dialogue? Look... I do not want to freak you out, but you are about to feel a bit under the weather.

Chapter 8 – Sick & Abroad!

Every time I travel abroad, I buy insurance, but the truth is I always hope I will not need it. Being sick can be scary, and no one likes to feel ill. Moreover, nobody wants it to interrupt their vacation! However, if you have to be prepared for something, this is definitely it. Great communication can be the key to solving major problems. So, let's get prepared.

| Ill | Enfermo |

| I think I am **ill**. | Creo que estoy **enfermo**. |

Here we see the word "n-ferh-moh" again, I know, but it is very important.

| Cold | Resfriado |
| I think I caught a **cold**. | Creo que cogí un **resfriado**. |

Rehs-free-ah-doh

| Cough | Tos |
| I have a slight **cough**. | Tengo un poco de **tos**. |

Tos

| Pain | Dolor |
| I took something for the **pain**. | Me tomé algo para el **dolor**. |

Doh-lohr

Practice those wide-open "o" sounds.

Migraine	Migraña
I have a **migraine**.	Tengo **migraña**.

Mee-grah-nia

Swollen	Hinchado
My throat is a bit **swollen**.	Mi garganta está un poco **hinchada**.

In-cha-dah

Call the doctor	Llamar al médico
Do you want to call the **doctor**?	¿Quieres llamar al **médico**?

Meh-dee-ko

Hearing the word "médico" can work as an emergency signal. Please, practice this one.

Meh-dee-ko

Emergency	Emergencia

| I have an **emergency.** | Tengo una **emergencia.** |

Eh-mer-hen-sia

| Feel | Siento |
| I **feel** a bit better. | Me **siento** un poco mejor. |

See-N-to

| Patient | Paciente |
| I am a **patient** of Dr. Castillo. | Soy un **paciente** del Dr. Castillo. |

Pah-See-N-teh

| Blood pressure | Presión sanguínea |
| The **blood pressure** is fine. | La **presión sanguínea** está bien. |

Preh-si-on san-ghee-ne-ah

| Pharmacy | Farmacia |

Where is the nearest **pharmacy**?	¿Dónde está la **farmacia** más cercana?

Similar to English: "phar-ma-cee-ah".

Prescription	Prescripción
I will need a **prescription.**	Voy a necesitar una **prescripción.**

Pres-krip-sion

Pills	Píldoras
How many **pills** do I need?	¿Cuántas **píldoras** necesito?

Peel-doh-rahs

We already did something similar to this in the airplane chapter, remember? So, as I have been saying, this knowledge is additive. You know English. You have done this before. You got it. Ready for practice?

Liam: *Hello! I would like to speak to Dr. Castillo.*

	Hola! Me gustaría hablar con el Dr. Castillo.
Secretary (secretaria):	*Good afternoon, sir. What is your name?*
	Buenas tardes, señor. ¿Cuál es su nombre?
Liam:	*I am Liam Smith. One of his patients.*
	Soy Liam Smith. Uno de sus pacientes.
Secretary:	*Good afternoon, sir. Why do you call today?*
	¿Cuál es el motivo de su llamada?
Liam:	*I have an emergency. My youngest son has a strong headache.*
	Tengo una emergencia. Mi hijo menor tiene un fuerte dolor de cabeza.
Secretary:	*Any other symptoms?*
	Algún otro síntoma?
Liam:	*38°C fever. Also complaints of abdominal pain.*
	Fiebre de 38°C. También se queja de dolor abdominal.
Secretary:	*Is he allergic to something?*

	¿Es alérgico a algo?
Liam:	Yes. To gluten.
	Sí. Al gluten.
Secretary:	Is he taking any prescriptions?
	¿Está tomando alguna prescripción?
Liam:	No, just a dietary supplement.
	No. Sólo un suplemento dietético.
Secretary:	Come here at once and bring those pills.
	Vengan aquí de inmediato y traigan esas píldoras.

Yeah, I know what you are thinking: no parent with a celiac kid would give him random pills! I feel you, but I have also seen it happen.

I truly hope my book is helping you. I am a travel and diversity lover, and I hope other people enjoy these experiences just as much. I know how much independence and confidence you can get by being able to communicate in more than one language. So, stay with me! We need you focused and optimistic! Did not I tell you? We need to go find you a job.

Chapter 9 – Learn the Ropes

Looking for new employment can be both a frustrating and an exciting situation. I am used to working on my own–which allows me to travel more–but I still have to get my own clients. If you are relocating or just thinking of spending a season in another city, finding a job at a local business could be a great opportunity to get in touch with the culture from a closer perspective.

As always, I will try to keep it simple.

Employment	Empleo
I am looking for **employment.**	Estoy buscando **empleo.**

M-pleh-oh

Employer	Jefe
My **employer** looks nice.	Mi **jefe** se ve agradable.

The most direct translation for "employer" is "empleador", but it is not very common to hear people say it that way.

He-feh

Employee	Empleado
I am an **employee** of this shop.	Soy un **empleado** de esta tienda.

M-pleh-ah-doh

Permanent position	Puesto fijo
I would like a **permanent position.**	Quisiera un **puesto fijo.**

Pooes-to-fee-jo

Temporary job	Trabajo temporal
I have a **temporary job.**	Tengo un **trabajo temporal.**

Trah-bah-joh-tem-po-rahl

Salary	Sueldo

| I want a **salary** increase. | Quiero un aumento de **sueldo.** |

Again, "salario" is the direct equivalent, but in terms of pronunciation and use, "sueldo" will perfectly do the work.

First and last name are very common expressions, and so far, you must have used it a dozen times. However, we will need it to write your CV, so just in case…

| First name | Nombre |
| What is your **first name**? | ¿Cuál es tu primer **nombre**? |

Nom-bre

| Last name | Apellido |
| My **last name** is Lopez. | Mi **apellido** es Lopez. |

Ah-peh-yi-doh

| Profession | Profesión |
| What is your **profession**? | ¿Cuál es tu **profesión**? |

Pro-phe-sion

Credentials	Credenciales
Here are my **credentials**.	Aquí están mis **credenciales**.

Kre-den-sia-les

Skills	Habilidades
These are my main **skills**.	Estas son mis **habilidades** principales.

Ah-bee-lee-da-des

As we know, the hiring criteria is changing. For many companies around the world, professions and studies are not as important as they used to be. Therefore, a very complete list of your most prominent skills will be important.

Job title	Título profesional
My **job title** is Manager.	Mi **título profesional** es Gerente.

Tee-too-loh-pro-phe-sio-nal

Job description	Descripción de rol
That is not under my **job description**.	Eso no está dentro de mi **descripción de rol**.

Des-krip-cion-the-rol

Your job description is, of course, crucial. While your job title might say something, your job description should provide a specific idea of what is expected from you.

Milestone	Hito
What is your favorite **milestone**?	¿Cuál es tu **hito** preferido?

Ee-toh

As you may know, where you have worked in the past and for how long are not as important anymore. What truly matters is what you got to accomplish while working with this or that during that time. Select your "hitos" to show for your skills.

Manager	Gerente
Congratulations! You are the new **manager**.	¡Felicidades! Eres el nuevo **gerente**.

N-kar-ga-doh

Congratulations! I am so happy for you!

That escalated quickly, huh?

You know my motto: practice makes perfect! Let's dive into our next dialogue.

Manager (gerente):	*Hello! What can I do for you?*
	¡Hola! ¿Qué puedo hacer por ti?
Owen:	*Hello! I am looking for employment.*
	¡Hola! Estoy buscando trabajo.
Manager	*What is your name?*
	¿Cuál es tu nombre?
Owen:	*Owen Miller.*
	Owen Miller.
Manager	*Very well. What type of work are you looking for?*
	Muy bien. ¿Qué clase de trabajo estás buscando?

Owen: *I would like anything. Even a temporary job.*

Me gustaría cualquier cosa. Incluso un trabajo temporal.

Manager *Right. Did you bring your CV?*

Correcto. ¿Trajiste tu CV?

Owen: *Yes. Here it is.*

Sí. Aquí está.

Manager *Very good. What are your major skills?*

Muy bien. ¿Cuáles son tu mayores habilidades?

Owen: *I am good at logo design.*

Soy bueno en diseño de logos.

Manager *What are your most relevant milestones from the past year?*

¿Cuáles son sus hitos más importantes del último año?

Owen: *I won campaigns for logo refreshments in 5 major companies.*

Gané campañas para refrescar el logo de 5 grandes empresas.

Manager	*All right. We will call you for another interview.*
	Muy bien. Te llamaremos para otra entrevista.
Owen:	*Do you have any vacancies?*
	¿Tienen ustedes alguna vacante?
Manager	*We have a job for a designer. It could turn into a permanent position.*
	Tenemos trabajo para un diseñador. Puede convertirse en un trabajo fijo.
Owen:	*That is great.*
	Eso es genial.
Manager	*Yes, it is. You would get an entry salary plus bonuses.*
	Sí, lo es. Obtendrías salario de entrada más bonos.
Owen:	*Awesome. I will wait for your call.*
	Increíble. Esperaré su llamada.

We have already had a little walkthrough for an interview, but we will work harder on that in the next chapter. After all, we have to get you ready for your first big job.

www.LearnLikeNatives.com

Chapter 10 – Bring, Learn & Lead

As the title for this chapter suggests, now is the time to bring, to learn, and to lead, because you have to shine in your job interview. For this, we will work in a new tense: the future. This is the moment to talk about ambition, show how good you are at planning and projecting, and demonstrate why you know you will be a great fit.

First verb: "to bring" – "aportar". As you will see, the root is "aport-".

Ah-por-tar

To bring	Aportar	Root	Termination
I will bring	Yo aportaré	Aport-	Ar changes to "aré"
You will bring	Tú aportarás		Ar changes to "arás"
He/She/It will bring	Él aportará		Ar changes to "ará"

We will bring	Nosotros aportaremos		Ar changes to "aremos"
You will bring	Ustedes aportarán		Ar changes to "arán"
They will bring	Ellos/Ellas aportarán		Ar changes to "arán"

The good thing is a job interview comes down to talking mostly about yourself. Therefore, it is important for you to know all the conjugations because you may want to talk about your plans for specific people or other departments. The main goal, however, is learning to talk about yourself.

Yo ah-por-tah-réh

Now, let's go through examples.

I will bring all my experience.	Yo aportaré toda mi experiencia.
He will bring many resources.	Él aportará muchos recursos.

We will bring a new selling strategy.	Nosotros aportaremos una nueva estrategia de ventas.
They will bring all the volunteers for this project.	Ellos aportarán todos los voluntarios para este proyecto.

It is time to go through our second termination: verbs that end in "-er".

Remember, you have to spot the root and then make the corresponding changes for every termination and conjugation. For the verb "aprender", the root is "aprend-".

To learn	Aprender	Root	Termination
I will learn	Yo aprenderé	Aprend-	Er changes to "eré"
You will learn	Tú aprenderás		Er changes to "erás"
He/She/It will learn	Él/Ella/Eso aprenderá		Er changes to "erá"
We will learn	Nosotros aprenderemos		Er changes to "eremos"

You will learn	Ustedes aprenderán		Er changes to "erán"
They will learn	Ellos/Ellas aprenderán		Er changes to "erán"

Again, let's take a moment to focus on you: ah-pren-deh-ré.

I will learn in this company.	Yo aprenderé dentro de esta compañía.
He will learn from this experience.	Él aprenderá con esta experiencia.
We will learn through hard work.	Nosotros aprenderemos a través del trabajo arduo.
They will learn a lot.	Ellos aprenderán mucho.

From a hiring perspective, "to lead" is a very important verb. Being able to lead is a well-appreciated skill for most recruiters, especially for some positions.

The root for the verb "dirigir" is "dirig-".

To lead	Dirigir	Root	Termination
I will lead	Yo dirigiré	Dirig-	Ir changes to "iré"
You will lead	Tú dirigirás		Ir changes to "irás"
He/She/It will lead	Él dirigirá		Ir changes to "irá"
We will lead	Nosotros dirigiremos		Ir changes to "iremos"
You will lead	Ustedes dirigirán		Ir changes to "irán"
They will lead	Ellos/Ellas dirigirán		Ir changes to "irán"

Yo-dee-ree-hee-reh

You will lead this project.	Tú dirigirás este proyecto.
She will lead this department.	Ella dirigirá este departamento.

We will lead the first part of the conference.	Nosotros dirigiremos la primera parte de la conferencia.
They will lead us to success.	Ellos nos dirigirán al éxito.

The next verb to look at is the verb "to be". It is with this verb that I first knew about the auxiliary for future (will) and its uses. More than that, it gives you a basic structure for putting sentences together in "futuro simple", the most commonly used tense for the future.

To be	**Ser**	**Estar**
I will be	Yo seré	Yo estaré
You will be	Tú serás	Tú estarás
He/She/It will be	Él será	Él estará
We will be	Nosotros seremos	Nosotros estaremos
You/They will be	Ustedes/Ellos/Ellas serán	Ustedes/Ellos/Ellas estarán

First, let's practice with the future tense of "ser".

I will be the leader in this project.	Yo seré el líder de este proyecto.
He will be a great asset to this team.	Él será un gran activo para este equipo.
This software will be great for us.	Este programa será genial para nosotros.
They will take care of everything.	Ellos se encargarán de todo.

Now, a few examples with the future tense of "estar".

I will be in a lead position this time.	Yo estaré en una posición de liderazgo esta vez.
He will be waiting for your instructions.	Él estará esperando por tus instrucciones.
This job will be waiting for you.	Este trabajo estará esperando por ti.
We will be in a meeting for the next hour.	Nosotros estaremos en una reunión por la próxima hora.

You can see that for Spanish, the words "will be" compress to form a simple idea: "seré o estaré". This is the Spanish form for "to be" that will happen in the future.

With this, you can create sentences talking about what you have planned for the future.

"With these changes, we will be the first company in our field."

"Con estos cambios, nosotros seremos la primera compañía en nuestro campo."

Now, let's check our final verb, "tener".

To have	**Tener**
I will have	Yo tendré
You will have	Tú tendrás
He/She/It will have	Él tendrá
We will have	Nosotros tendremos
You will have	Ustedes tendrán
They will have	Ellos/Ellas tendrán

"To have" is a great verb because it helps us build new tenses, as you have seen. In this case, we can use it in two ways: first, as the "future simple" form for having. Alternatively, you can use it to create the "future perfect", or "futuro perfecto", a tense that helps you indicate something that will happen somewhere between now and another point in the future. I should show you an example.

"I will have it ready by 2 pm."

"Lo tendré listo para las 2 pm."

This is a sentence using "futuro simple".

Pronoun + verb future.

"I will have done this by 2 pm."

"Lo habré terminado para las 2 pm."

This is a sentence written in "futuro perfecto".

Pronoun + "to have" in future + past participle.

This mix of future and past tense verbs create the complexity of the "future perfect".

I will have everything done by tonight.	Yo tendré todo listo para esta noche.
You will have been here for 2 years in one week.	Tú habrás estado aquí por dos años en una semana.
She will have made it if she passes this.	Ella lo habrá logrado si aprueba esto.
They will have done it by the weekend.	Ellos habrán hecho esto para el fin.

Yes. I can almost hear you talking. No worries. We will see more of these examples in the next dialogue.

Mr. King (Sr. King): *Hello. Are you Leo Mitchell?*

Hola. ¿Tú eres Leo Mitchell?

Leo: *Good afternoon. Yes, I am.*

Buenas tardes. Sí, lo soy.

Mr. King (Sr. King): *Perfect. Please, come with me.*

Perfecto. Por favor, ven conmigo.

Leo: *Sure.*

Seguro.

Mr. King (Sr. King): *Tell me, Leo. If we hire you, what will you bring to the company?*

Dime, Leo. Si te contratamos, ¿qué aportarás a la compañía?

Leo: *I will bring 10-year experience in conflict and risk management.*

Aportaré 10 años de experiencia en manejo de riesgos y conflicto.

Mr. King (Sr. King): *According to your knowledge, when will the updates be made?*

De acuerdo a tu conocimiento, ¿cuándo estarán hechas las actualizaciones?

Leo: *I will have updates done within the first semester of 2020.*

Tendré las actualizaciones listas durante el primer semestre de 2020.

Mr. King (Sr. King): *What will you need to achieve that?*

¿Qué necesitarás para conseguir eso?

Leo: *I will need a team, including two technicians.*

Necesitaré un equipo, incluidos dos técnicos.

www.LearnLikeNatives.com

Mr. King (Sr. King):	*Very well. When will you start?* Muy bien. ¿Cuándo comenzarás?
Leo:	*Next week will be okay.* La semana que viene estará bien.

I hope you are cracking this. All languages are about structure and, even if some are more complex than others, they become natural with time and practice. By the way, have you had a look at your new office?

Chapter 11 – New Job, New Life

I always get nervous on my first day working at a new place. But I think it is also exciting to meet new people, form new alliances, and basically have the chance to network in unknown circles.

Nervous or not, we are here to prepare you for what is coming. Do you want to join me?

Please, follow me into your new job.

Office	Oficina
This is your **office.**	Esta es tu **oficina.**

Oh-fee-si-nah

www.LearnLikeNatives.com

Computer	Computador
Your **computer** is ready to use.	Tu **computador** está listo para usar.

Kom-poo-tah-dor

Database	Base de datos
I granted you access to this **database.**	Te di acceso a esta **base de datos.**

Bah-se-the-da-tos

Yes! You are right! All of these expressions are similar to the ones you use! It will be a piece of cake!

Software	Programa
We have the best **software** to manage our database.	Tenemos el mejor **programa** para manejar nuestra base de datos.

Pro-gra-ma

Keyboard	Teclado

This is a nice **keyboard.**	Este es un buen **teclado.**

Teh-kla-doh

Monitor	Monitor
I need a larger **monitor.**	Necesito un **monitor** más grande.

Mo-ni-tor

The only difference between this word in English and in Spanish is where you put the accents in. While the stronger syllable in English is "mo", in Spanish it is in "tor". Remember to use a clear "t" to pronounce this.

Mouse	Ratón
My **mouse** is ergonomic.	Mi **ratón** es ergonómico.

Ra-tón

Hard drive	Disco duro
That is a 2 terabyte **hard drive.**	Ese es un **disco duro** de 2 terabyte.

This-coh-duh-roh

File	Archivo
You will find all that you need in the **file**.	Encontrarás todo lo que necesitas en el **archivo**.

R-chi-vo

Document	Documento
I already sent that **document**.	Ya envié ese **documento**.

Do-cu-men-to

Report	Informe
I will send the **report** this afternoon.	Enviaré el **informe** esta tarde.

In-for-meh

Coordinate	Coordinar
We need to **coordinate** that meeting.	Necesitamos **coordinar** esa reunión.

Kor-di-nar

Desk	Escritorio
This is a nice **desk**.	Este es un buen **escritorio**.

S-kri-toh-rio

Department	Departamento
I work for the Human Resources **department**.	Yo trabajo para el **departamento** de Recursos Humanos.

The-par-ta-men-to

Coworker	Compañero de trabajo
I had lunch with a **coworker**.	Almorcé con un **compañero de trabajo**.

Kom-pa-nie-ro the tra-bah-joh

See how many of these words are almost the same as English words, just with some small shifts?

Are you eager to practice? Great! Let's do this!

Eli: *How do you like your new office?*

¿Qué te parece tu nueva oficina?

Jace: *I like it a lot. I think I will need another monitor to split screens.*

Me gusta mucho. Creo que necesitaré otro monitor para dividir pantallas.

Eli: *Most coworkers do. We can coordinate that with the IT Department.*

La mayoría de los compañeros de trabajo lo hace. Podemos coordinarlo con el Departamento de tecnología.

Jace: *Perfect. Thank you. I love my desk.*

Perfecto. Gracias. Me encanta my escritorio.

Eli: *Yes. We invest in computers, software, and great equipment.*

Sí. Invertimos en computadores, programas y grandes equipos.

Jace: *When are you expecting to have the files you requested?*

¿Cuándo esperas tener los archivos que pediste?

Eli: *Tomorrow is fine.*

Mañana está bien.

Jace: *Good. I just have to add a few documents.*

Bien. Sólo tengo que agregar un par de documentos.

Eli: *Great, Jace! I think you will be a great addition to our team.*

¡Genial, Jace! Creo que serás una gran adición a nuestro equipo.

Jace: *Thank you for trusting in me. I will not let you down*

Gracias por confiar en mí. No te defraudaré.

How did you like your first day at the new office? Already familiar with the coffee machine? You should better get to work because now you have some big projects coming.

www.LearnLikeNatives.com

A Quick Message

A quick message before we start the final chapter of this book.

"No one can whistle a symphony. It takes a whole orchestra to play it." –

H.E. Luccock

Do you want to be part of the orchestra of the Learning Spanish community?

Here is how:

If you're enjoying this book, I would like to kindly ask you to leave a brief review on Amazon.

Reviews aren't easy to come by, but they have a profound impact in supporting my work. This way, I can keep creating new content to help the whole community at my very best.

I would be incredibly thankful if you could just take a minute to leave a quick review on Amazon, even if it's just a sentence or two!

It's that simple!

Thank you so much for taking the time to leave a short review on Amazon.

The community and I are very appreciative, as your review makes a difference.

Now, let's get back to learning Spanish

www.LearnLikeNatives.com

Chapter 12 – Bringing Home the Bacon

You have been preparing for this moment. You got yourself a new job, you have a new office and work team, and now is the time to start closing some business and bringing home the money. As always, let's first go with the essentials.

Meeting	Reunión
We have everything ready for the **meeting.**	Tenemos todo listo para la **reunión.**

Re-u-nion

Sell	Vender
We plan to **sell** when it reaches $95.	Nosotros planeamos **vender** cuando alcance $95.

Ven-der

Take your time to practice that final "r" sound.

Capital	Capital

| We need to raise **capital.** | Necesitamos recaudar **capital.** |

Ka-pi-tal

| Market | Mercado |
| The **market** is shifting. | El **mercado** está cambiando. |

Mer-ka-doh

How are your open vowels looking? "Ah" is a good sound to practice.

| Stock market | Bolsa de valores |
| The **stock market** could crash. | La **bolsa de valores** podría colapsar. |

Bol-sa the va-lo-res

| Project | Proyecto |
| The new **project** is very complex. | El nuevo **proyecto** es bastante complejo. |

Pro-jec-toh

www.LearnLikeNatives.com

Budget	Presupuesto
The available **budget** is 750k.	El **presupuesto** disponible es de 750k.

Pre-su-pooes-to

Presentation	Presentación
I'll have the **presentation** ready by 1 pm.	Tendré la **presentación** lista a la 1 pm.

Pre-sen-ta-sion

Supply	Oferta
The **supply** is decreasing for some commodities.	La **oferta** está disminuyendo para algunos productos básicos.

Offer-ta

Demand	Demanda
The people **demand** new solutions.	La gente **demanda** nuevas soluciones.

De-man-da

Experience	Experiencia
I have 7 years of professional **experience.**	Tengo 7 años de **experiencia** profesional.

Ex-pe-riehn-sia

Invoice	Factura
I will send you my **invoice.**	Te enviaré mi **factura.**

Fact-oo-ra

Credit	Crédito
They have great **credit.**	Ellos tienen un gran **crédito.**

Cré-di-to

Just like the English word, but you add a final "o".

Loan	Préstamo
I will pay half of the **loan.**	Yo pagaré la mitad del **préstamo.**

Pres-tah-moh

Taxes	Impuestos
I have to calculate my **taxes.**	Tengo que calcular mis **impuestos.**

Im-pooes-tohs

Investment	Inversión
It is a great **investment.**	Es una gran **inversión.**

In-ver-sion

Spend	Gastar
It is important to **spend** in quality.	Es importante **gastar** en calidad.

Gas-tar

Save	Ahorrar
We can **save** up to 30%.	Podemos **ahorrar** hasta un 30%.

Ah-ho-rrar

Lose	Perder
Sometimes you need to **lose**.	A veces necesitas **perder**.

Per-der

Here we are. This is the final test. This chapter's practice is meant to gather general knowledge from the last three chapters. Are you ready to buckle? Don't be scared. You got this.

Mr. Reed (Sr. Reed):	*I am going to be clear: I want a company to protect my investment.*
	Yo voy a ser claro: quiero una compañía que proteja mi inversión.
Mr. Evans:	*Perfect. I can offer you all my experience for that job.*
	Perfecto. Puedo ofrecerte toda mi experiencia para ese trabajo.
Mr. Reed:	*What will be your strategy?*
	¿Cuál será tu estrategia?
Mr. Evans:	*You have good credit. I plan to use a loan and increase the supply.*

	Ustedes poseen buen crédito. Planeo usar un préstamo para aumentar la oferta.
Mr. Reed:	*How will I save capital that way?*
	¿Cómo ahorraré capital de esa manera?
Mr. Evans:	*By covering for the demand, I expect a rise in the Stock Market.*
	Al cubrir la demanda, espero un alza en la Bolsa de Valores.
Mr. Reed:	*That will not do it alone.*
	Solo eso no lo logrará.
Mr. Evans:	*I know. That is why we have a strategy to increase our market share by 3%.*
	Lo sé. Por eso tenemos una estrategia para incrementar su cuota de mercado en un 3%.
Mr. Reed:	*Very well. I expect that you will have a great presentation for my board meeting.*
	Muy bien. Espero que tengas una gran presentación para mi reunión de junta.
Mr. Evans:	*You know I will. My budget projections do not lie.*

Tú sabes que sí. Mis proyecciones de presupuesto no mienten.

Mr. Reed: *All right. I expect your invoice, then.*

Muy bien. Espero tu factura, entonces.

Mr. Evans: *I will be sending it tomorrow.*

La estaré enviando mañana.

I want to know your opinion. How was this practice for you? Ask yourself, how can you improve? As I have been saying from the beginning, it is up to you to master these phrases and words. And practice is the only way to do it--talking and listening, repeatedly.

Conclusion

Congratulations on making it through to the end of this book! You now have all the tools you need to achieve your Spanish goals.

This is no science. Of course, there is a method, but it is mostly practicing, repeating, and doing! So, go for it. If you find yourself feeling unsure about something, just come back and look it up, and we'll go through it together! Yet, I am sure you already know so much, even more than you realize!

Look at all the things we did: we learned how to plan a trip, we discussed how to act if you or your family get sick, reviewed how to move around the city, ask for directions, and we had a nice conversation about how to talk about the past and the future.

We also learned how to deal with business in Spanish: we talked about how to present a CV and become an employee. Also, we went through some commercial and business Spanish to help you make great deals if you find yourself covering a management position.

Do you realize all the new things you can communicate now? You now have more resources for survival and regular living in a completely new environment, and I want to give you a big pat on the back for coming this far.

You can find the rest of the books in the series, as well as a whole host of other resources, at LearnLikeNatives.com. Simply add the book to your library to take the next step in your language learning journey. If you are ever in need of new ideas or direction, refer to our 'Speak Like a Native' eBook, available to you for free at LearnLikeNatives.com, which clearly outlines practical steps you can take to continue learning any language you choose.

Nevertheless, did I mention we are not over yet?

Now the fun part begins: try to watch in Spanish your favorite cartoons, or try with some famous TV series, of course with Spanish subtitles (yes Spanish subtitles, you can make it!). I would advise you, *Ugly Betty* (in Spanish, it is called *Betty la Fea*). It's a big classic, easy, and fun to follow, yet extremely helpful for improving your Spanish!

Again, thank you for reading. I hope to meet you in the near future so we can learn even more!

www.LearnLikeNatives.com

www.LearnLikeNatives.com

Learn Like a Native is a revolutionary **language education brand** that is taking the linguistic world by storm. Forget boring grammar books that never get you anywhere, Learn Like a Native teaches you languages in a fast and fun way that actually works!

As an international, multichannel, language learning platform, we provide **books, audio guides and eBooks** so that you can acquire the knowledge you need, swiftly and easily.

Our **subject-based learning**, structured around real-world scenarios, builds your conversational muscle and ensures you learn the content most relevant to your requirements.
Discover our tools at *LearnLikeNatives.com*

When it comes to learning languages, we've got you covered!

www.ingramcontent.com/pod-product-compliance
Lightning Source LLC
Chambersburg PA
CBHW070043120526
44589CB00035B/2302